ar rd Lo

ROMAN SITES

John Malam

a Capstone company — publishers for children

Raintree is an imprint of Capstone Global Library Limited, a company incorporated in England and Wales having its registered office at 264 Banbury Road, Oxford, OX2 7DY – Registered company number: 6695582

www.raintree.co.uk

myorders@raintree.co.uk

Produced for Raintree by

White-Thomson Publishing Ltd

+44 (0)1273 477 216

www.wtpub.co.uk

Edited by Sonya Newland
Designed by Rocket Design (East Anglia) Ltd
Original illustrations © Capstone Global Library Ltd 2017
Illustrated by Ron Dixon
Production by Duncan Gilbert
Originated by Capstone Global Library Ltd
Printed and bound in China

ISBN 978 1 4747 5412 5
21 20 19 18 17
10 9 8 7 6 5 4 3 2 1

British Library Cataloguing in Publication Data
A full catalogue record for this book is available from the British Library.

Acknowledgements
We would like to thank the following for permission to reproduce photographs:
Adam Stanford © Aerial-Cam Ltd.: 15, 17, 29; Alamy: Heritage Image Partnership, 16, 19 top, Powered by Light/ Alan Spencer, 7, A.P.S. (UK), 8, Robert Estall, 10, Robert Harding, 5 top, Skyscan Photolibrary, 11; iStock: craigb40, 14 bottom; John Malam: 27 bottom; Courtesy of the Portable Antiquities Scheme: 19 bottom (ID: NMS-53FAA7), 27 top (ID: LON-9365A3); Shutterstock: abxyz, 4, Alexey Lobanov, 18, Chris Dorney, 25, Chrispo, 28, Davidolfi, 20, jeafish Ping, 22–23, Juan Aunion, 23, Laurence Gough, 26, Leckchalit, 21, Michael Conrad, 12, Neil Mitchell, 9, Nicola Pulham, 24, Paul J Martin, 6 bottom, Phillip Maguire, cover, SueC, 14 top.

We would like to thank Philip Parker for his help in the preparation of this book.

Every effort has been made to contact copyright holders of material reproduced in this book. Any omissions will be rectified in subsequent printings if notice is given to the publisher.

CONTENTS

Some words are shown in bold, **like this**. You can
find out what they mean by looking in the glossary.

THE ROMANS IN BRITAIN

In the summer of AD 43, about 40,000 Roman soldiers set sail from northern France. Their ships crossed the English Channel, and in a few hours they reached their landing place. The Roman invasion of Britain had begun.

Why did the Romans invade?

At the time of the invasion, the Roman **emperor** was Claudius (10 BC–AD 54). To show how powerful he was, Claudius decided to add new land to the **Roman Empire**. He ordered the mighty Roman army to **conquer** Britain.

Emperor Claudius ordered the Roman invasion of Britain in AD 43.

DIG DEEPER

** CAESAR'S EXPEDITIONS **

Nearly 100 years before Claudius became emperor, the Roman general Julius Caesar made two **expeditions** to Britain. He arrived with an army in 55 BC and then again in 54 BC. He took hostages, and the British agreed to pay a **tribute** to the Romans each year. After this, Caesar left Britain, never to return.

Taking control

Archaeologists believe that the Romans landed at Richborough, in east Kent, where they built a camp. From there, Roman soldiers marched north. Within a few weeks they had captured the town of Camulodunum (present-day Colchester, Essex). Emperor Claudius was there to see the victory, and it was said that the kings of 11 different tribes surrendered to him. The Roman invasion of Britain had got off to a good start.

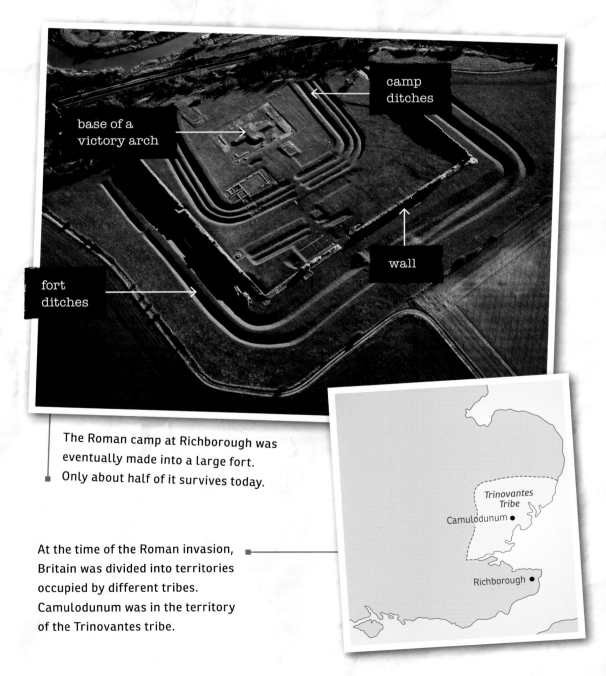

camp ditches

base of a victory arch

fort ditches

wall

The Roman camp at Richborough was eventually made into a large fort. Only about half of it survives today.

At the time of the Roman invasion, Britain was divided into territories occupied by different tribes. Camulodunum was in the territory of the Trinovantes tribe.

Trinovantes Tribe

Camulodunum ●

Richborough ●

Advance into Wales

By about AD 47, the Romans controlled most of southern and central Britain. They then began to advance into what is now Wales, but their progress was slow. In AD 60, the Romans captured the island of Anglesey, off the northwestern coast of Wales. It seemed everything was going to plan – but then came bad news.

In AD 60–61, British tribes rebelled against the Roman invaders. They were led by Boudicca, queen of the Iceni tribe. Her forces burned the Roman towns of Camulodunum (Colchester), Londinium (London) and Verulamium (St Albans).

Boudicca's army burned three Roman towns to the ground. Her army was then defeated in a battle.

This famous statue of Boudicca in her war chariot is in London.

BRIGANTES

Mona (Anglesey)

PARISI

DECEANGLI

Battle fought in central Britain

Romans

ORDOVICES

CORITANI

Camulodunum (Colchester, provincial capital of Roman Britain)

ICENI

CATUVELLAUNI

British tribes

TRINOVANTES

Verulamium (St Albans)

Londinium (London)

DUMNONII

DUROTRIGES

ATREBATE

The British are beaten

At the time of the British **rebellion**, most of the Roman army was in North Wales. When news of the disaster reached them, 10,000 Roman soldiers marched south to fight the British. In the battle that followed, the British were defeated and Boudicca took her own life. The Romans rebuilt the towns that had been destroyed in the rebellion, and the tribes of Britain accepted that the Romans were there to stay.

Re-enactors show how the Romans and Queen Boudicca's army fought each other hand-to-hand.

DIG DEEPER

** BOUDICCA, THE WARRIOR QUEEN **

The Roman writer Dio Cassius described Boudicca. He said she was very tall, had a terrifying appearance, a harsh voice, and long red hair to her hips. She wore a gold necklace and a dress of many colours. She shook a spear that scared all who saw her.

WATLING STREET

Before the Romans, there were almost no proper roads in Britain. Instead, there were trackways. These were well-used routes that could be muddy and bumpy. When the Romans arrived, they began building roads that were paved with pebbles and stone. Some Roman roads are still in use today.

WATLING STREET

Lifelines for the army

By about AD 150, the Romans had built 16,000 kilometres (10,000 miles) of roads in Britain. At first, the roads were supply routes for the army. They linked towns and forts, and all the supplies the army needed were transported on these roads. Later, **merchants** and traders began to use the roads. They took goods to towns and villages across Britain.

WHAT: Roman road

WHERE: from Richborough, Kent, to Wroxeter, Shropshire

WHEN: begun about AD 45

The busy Edgware Road in London is part of the Roman Watling Street (see page 9).

From coast to country

The first major Roman road in Britain went from Richborough in Kent, to an army camp at Viroconium, Shropshire (present-day Wroxeter). It covered a distance of about 370 km (230 miles). The road's old name is Watling Street. Today, the A2 and A5 roads follow its route.

Dere Street Roman road ran north from Eboracum (York) to the Antonine Wall in Scotland.

DIG DEEPER

** HOW TO SPOT A ROMAN ROAD **

Look for long, straight roads. The Romans built straight roads because they were the shortest route between two places. If the road leads somewhere with a name ending with -caster, -chester or -cester (from the Latin *castrum*, meaning "military camp"), then it is probably a Roman road. These towns and cities include Lancaster, Chester, Manchester, Leicester and Gloucester.

364 km (226 miles) long

CAERLEON FORTRESS

As the Romans advanced across Britain, they built many forts for the soldiers to live in. In some places, extra-large forts were built. Each one was a **fortress** for a **legion** of Roman soldiers. A legion had about 5,000 men in it.

Show of strength

Britain's three permanent Roman fortresses were at Deva (Chester), Eboracum (York), and in South Wales at Isca (Caerleon, near Newport). The Roman army began building the fortress at Caerleon in about AD 74. The **legionaries** based there were from the Second Augusta Legion. They built Caerleon fortress on land belonging to the Silures, the most powerful tribe in South Wales. The fortress showed the Silures – and surrounding tribes – how strong the Roman army was.

CAERLEON FORTRESS

WHAT: army fortress
WHERE: Caerleon, south Wales
WHEN: begun about AD 74

barracks

sewer

toilet block

Barracks at Caerleon were divided into small rooms for the soldiers.

Inside the fortress

Caerleon fortress was rectangular in shape, with rounded corners (Roman forts are said to have a "playing-card" shape). At first it was made of earth and timber, but later it was strengthened with walls of stone. In the centre was a building that served as its headquarters. Around this were the barrack blocks, where the soldiers lived. There was also a hospital building, workshops, baths and toilet blocks.

DIG DEEPER

** THE AMPHITHEATRE **

Outside Caerleon fortress is an **amphitheatre**. **Archaeologists** believe that this large open-air building was used by soldiers as a training or parade ground. It might also have been used by **gladiators** for fighting contests.

spectators sat here →

Caerleon amphitheatre had seats for about 6,000 people.

display area

entrance

HADRIAN'S WALL

The Romans had hoped to **conquer** the whole of Britain, but this plan failed. Instead, they ended up building a wall to mark the northern frontier of the **Roman Empire**. This was Hadrian's Wall, and it is the greatest Roman structure in Britain.

HADRIAN'S WALL

Why build the wall?

In AD 118, tribes in the north rebelled against the Roman invaders. The Romans defeated the rebels, but northern Britain was becoming a difficult area to control. The **emperor** Hadrian (AD 76–138) decided to build a wall to separate the unruly northern Britons from the "civilised" people of the Roman world.

WHAT: frontier wall
WHERE: northern England
WHEN: begun AD 122

Hadrian's Wall was originally about 6 metres (20 feet) high.

milecastle (50 soldiers based here)

Hadrian's Wall

Building the wall

In AD 122, Roman soldiers began building Hadrian's Wall using stone, turf and timber. It took about 10 years to complete the wall. The finished wall crossed northern Britain from coast to coast – 117 km (73 miles). Seventeen forts were built along the wall, each housing 500–1,000 Roman soldiers. In between the forts were gateways where soldiers stood guard. They are called milecastles because they were built one Roman mile apart from each other (1,000 paces). On either side of the wall were deep ditches.

DIG DEEPER

** THE ANTONINE WALL **

In AD 138, Antoninus Pius (AD 86–161) became Roman emperor. He wanted to expand the Roman Empire in Britain by conquering the land north of Hadrian's Wall, in present-day Scotland. However, he too ended up building a wall to mark the Roman Empire's northern edge. It was named the Antonine Wall, after the emperor.

Firth of Forth

Antonine Wall
Begun in AD 142

North Sea

Hadrian's Wall
Begun in AD 122

Irish Sea

The Antonine Wall runs across central Scotland.

Soldiers

The Roman Empire was vast, and the Roman soldiers working on Hadrian's Wall came from many different lands. There were men from present-day Spain, France, the Netherlands, Belgium and Germany. They had many duties to carry out. These included collecting supplies from the stores, delivering mail, going out on patrol, guard duty and building work. Soldiers needed to be fit and healthy. They practised fighting. They also went on long marches in full uniform, carrying their weapons, cooking equipment and food with them.

Modern actors dressed as Roman soldiers, showing a formation called a testudo, or tortoise.

Soldiers from warmer parts of the Roman Empire had to get used to the cold winters of northern England.

Hadrian's Wall

Civilians

Many civilians also lived along Hadrian's Wall in small settlements built outside the forts. If a soldier was married, this is where his wife and family might live. These settlements were like mini-towns. There were shops, workshops and temples. When soldiers had free time, this is where they went.

DIG DEEPER

** THE VINDOLANDA WRITING TABLETS **

Vindolanda is a large fort near Hadrian's Wall. Buried in its waterlogged soil, **archaeologists** found **writing tablets** dating from about AD 100, with traces of handwriting still on them. One Roman grumbles about the lack of beer; another is sent socks, sandals and underpants. There is even an invitation to a birthday party. As for the British, a Roman writer calls them "wretched Britons".

fort, with "playing-card" shape

civilian settlement outside fort

Stanegate Roman road

Vindolanda was a major fort that defended an important road called Stanegate near Hadrian's Wall.

WROXETER

One of the largest Roman towns in Britain by size lies beneath the fields of Shropshire, close to the River Severn. The Romans called it Viroconium. We know the village that stands there today as Wroxeter.

From fort to city

By around AD 60, the Roman army had reached the territory of the Cornovii tribe. The Cornovii's homeland was in the present-day county of Shropshire. Watling Street crossed the tribe's land. Near to where the road reached the River Severn, the Romans built a fort. They called it Viroconium. In about AD 90, the army moved out, and Viroconium grew into a city.

WROXETER

WHAT: city
WHERE: near Shrewsbury, Shropshire
WHEN: from about AD 90

This is how the Roman city of Viroconium (Wroxeter) might have looked in the AD 200s.

Busy city

The city covered about 81 hectares (200 acres). In the AD 200s, as many as 15,000 people lived there. Like many Roman cities, Viroconium was built on a grid pattern with roads and side streets dividing it into blocks. Inside the blocks were houses, a market hall, a bathhouse, a temple, workshops and a market square. The city was surrounded by a wall.

Romans entered the baths at Viroconium through large doors in the centre of this wall.

hot room

warm room

cold room

entrance to baths

DIG DEEPER

** LONDINIUM **

Soon after the Roman invasion of Britain, a settlement grew up at a crossing-place on the River Thames. The Romans named it Londinium. It became the capital of Roman Britain. Today, it is the city of London.

Towns: a new way of life

Before the Romans came to Britain, people lived in villages and on farms. The Romans introduced a whole new way of life – living in towns. By about AD 100, many towns had been built, and British people had moved to them. The Romans encouraged the native Britons to accept Roman ways. Here are some of the first towns in Roman Britain, and the approximate dates they began:

Colchester (Camulodunum), AD 43

London (Londinium), AD 43

St Albans (Verulamium), AD 43

Cirencester (Corinium Dobunnorum), AD 75

Exeter (Isca Dumnoniorum), AD 75

Caerwent (Venta Silurum), AD 78

Lincoln (Lindum), AD 80

Winchester (Venta Belgarum), AD 90

Wroxeter (Viroconium), AD 90

Gloucester (Glevum), AD 97

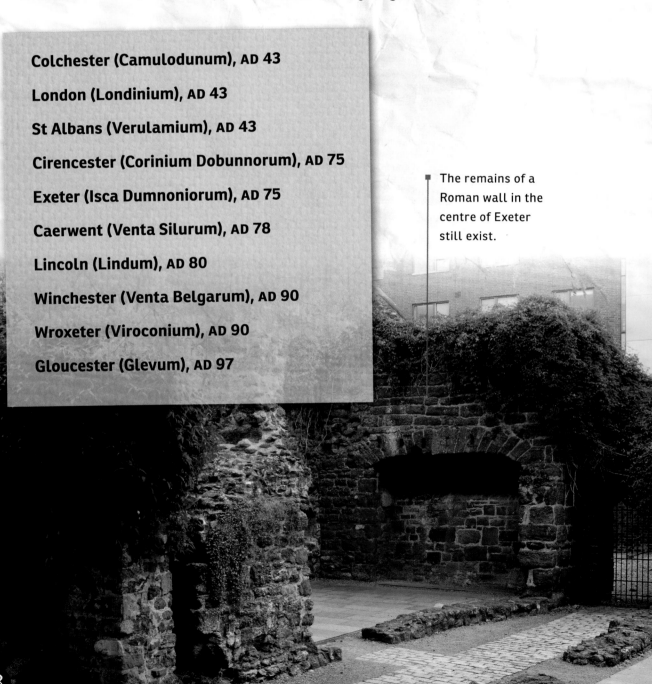

The remains of a Roman wall in the centre of Exeter still exist.

Along the high street

Silchester, Berkshire, is a good example of a Roman town. In Roman times it was known as Calleva Atrebatum. At its centre was the **forum**, or market square, where **merchants** sold fresh food and everyday goods. Along the streets were bakers' and butchers' shops and workshops for craftspeople. Elsewhere at Calleva was a rest-house for travellers, baths and an **amphitheatre**.

This is how the forum at Calleva Atrebatum (Silchester) might have looked in the AD 300s, surrounded by shops and houses.

DIG DEEPER

** INTERNATIONAL CURRENCY **

Coins were used in Britain before the Romans, but they came into everyday use under the Romans. Roman coins could be used anywhere in the **Roman Empire**.

This silver Roman coin was found in Norfolk in 2017. It shows **Emperor** Hadrian.

ROMAN BATHS, BATH

In south-west Britain, the Romans found a place where hot water came to the surface from a **spring**. They believed that the water had healing powers, and they set about putting it to use.

ROMAN BATHS

Healing water

Today we call this place Bath, but to the Romans it was Aquae Sulis. It means "the waters of Sulis". The local Britons believed the warm water was sacred to Sulis. Sulis was a goddess of healing, like the Roman goddess Minerva. The Romans dedicated their temple at Bath to the goddess "Sulis Minerva", which pleased both Britons and Romans.

WHAT: temple and baths
WHERE: Bath, Somerset
WHEN: AD 60-70

The Great Bath still fills with hot water from a natural spring. The Romans had a roof over it.

DIG DEEPER

** UNDERFLOOR HEATING **

Connected to the Roman baths was a furnace, which burned wood. The hot air from the furnace moved under the floor and up through hollow bricks behind the walls. This is how warmth entered the rooms and heated the water.

Taking the plunge

Visitors to the baths walked into the entrance hall. From there, they could see the sacred spring. They undressed in the changing room, then went into the warm room. From there they moved into the hot room and sat in the steam or took a bath in very hot water. Then they went to the cold pool for a swim before going back to the changing room to dry and dress themselves again.

long hair

Staring out from the temple of Sulis Minerva was this carving of a fearsome Briton.

moustache

CHESTER AMPHITHEATRE

Around Britain are the remains of about 20 Roman **amphitheatres**. Crowds gathered at these large, open-air buildings to watch spectacular shows. Soldiers also trained in the amphitheatres.

CHESTER AMPHITHEATRE

Largest in Britain

The Roman army built a **fortress** in north-west Britain at Deva (Chester) in about AD 76. This was a superb location for a military base. From there, the Romans could control North Wales and central Britain. Just outside the fortress walls, the Romans built the largest amphitheatre in Britain. It was a massive oval building, made of stone, with seats for about 8,000 people.

WHAT: amphitheatre
WHERE: Chester, Cheshire
WHEN: AD 70s

Only part of Chester's Roman amphitheatre has been uncovered.

seats

arena

Blood on the floor

Because the amphitheatre stood next to the fortress, **archaeologists** think it was used by Roman soldiers. It served as their training ground, where they practised battle movements and using their weapons. Soldiers might have held parades there. But the amphitheatre was also where the public came to watch animal fights, animal hunts and **gladiators** fighting.

Secutor gladiator armed with helmet and shield

Retiarius gladiator armed with net and trident

Gladiators like these present-day actors might have fought at Chester's amphitheatre.

DIG DEEPER

** GLADIATORS **

Gladiators were trained fighters who entertained crowds across the **Roman Empire**. There were many different types of gladiator. Some fought with nets and spears, others had swords and shields. Some wore armour, and some did not. Gladiator fights were a popular form of entertainment in Roman times.

ST ALBANS THEATRE

St Albans, which the Romans called Verulamium, grew up alongside the major road known as Watling Street (see page 8). It became a leading town with many grand buildings.

Out of the ashes

In Roman times, many buildings were made of wood, so fire was always a threat. Verulamium was burned to the ground twice. The first fire was in AD 61, when Boudicca destroyed the town (see page 6). The second fire was in about AD 155. Each fire gave the town authorities the chance to rebuild on a grander scale. After the second fire, they decided the town needed a theatre.

ST ALBANS THEATRE

WHAT: theatre
WHERE: St Albans, Hertfordshire
WHEN: about AD 155

The Roman theatre at Verulamium was in the shape of a semicircle.

Watling Street Roman road

scenery platform

seats

orchestra (performance area)

Laugh or cry?

The theatre at Verulamium is the most complete Roman theatre in Britain. On special days, actors performed plays on the floor of the orchestra. Some plays were funny (comedies). Others were sad (tragedies). At a sell-out show, as many as 5,000 people sat on wooden seats in the open air. They clicked their fingers and clapped their hands if they enjoyed it. They hissed if they didn't!

DIG DEEPER

** TOWN WALLS **

Many Roman towns in Britain had walls around them. These were to defend the town and its people. At Verulamium, the wall was about 6 m (20 ft) high, and 3.2 km (2 miles) long. There were two main gateways, and **watchtowers** were built along it.

Part of the Roman wall at Verulamium is still standing.

BIGNOR ROMAN VILLA

Some of the most impressive Roman remains in Britain have been found by accident. This is how a Roman villa was discovered in 1811, when a farmer was ploughing his field.

BIGNOR VILLA

Under the soil

George Tupper's plough struck something hard buried in the ground, so he stopped to clear away the soil. As he did, he uncovered a **mosaic** – a picture made from tiny cubes of coloured stone. It was on the floor of a room. This turned out to be one of many rooms in a Roman villa, all decorated with colourful mosaics.

WHAT: villa
WHERE: near Arundel, West Sussex
WHEN: about AD 200

The mosaic picture at Bignor shows Medusa – a creature with a woman's head and poisonous snakes for hair.

Grand designs

The mosaics at the Bignor Roman villa are some of the finest and most complete mosaics in Britain. There are scenes of **gladiators** fighting, the Roman goddess Venus, and a dolphin swimming. Others are patterns made from lines, triangles and squares. Above one mosaic are the letters TER. **Archaeologists** think these could be the initials for the craftsman who made the mosaic, signing it as an artist signs a picture. He may have been Tertius, Terentius or Tertullus.

This fragment from a large mosaic shows cubes of red, black and white stone set into a bed of mortar. This piece was found in London.

DIG DEEPER

** ROMAN VILLAS **

Villas were Roman houses or farms in the countryside. The largest villas, such as the one at Bignor, were big country houses at the centre of huge estates. They were places where workers grew wheat, barley and other crops for sale in nearby towns.

a replica of a Roman villa at the city of Viroconium (Wroxeter)

THE END OF ROMAN BRITAIN

Starting in the AD 250s, Roman soldiers gradually withdrew from Britain. They were sent away to defend the **frontiers** in other parts of the **Roman Empire**. This left Britain exposed and weak.

Arrival of the Saxons

At about the same time as Roman soldiers began to leave, **Saxon** raiders from northern Europe arrived. In an attempt to defend Britain, the Romans had built 11 great forts around the eastern and southern coasts, from Brancaster, Norfolk, to Portchester, Hampshire. **Archaeologists** call them Saxon Shore Forts. But the Roman defence plan did not work. By AD 410, the last of the Roman soldiers had left Britain and almost 400 years of Roman control of Britain came to an end.

There were no more **gladiators** or plays to watch, the public baths stopped working and grass grew in the streets. Roman towns and **villas** became ruins. Coins and even pottery went out of use. The Saxons brought their own way of life with them, and a new and exciting period in Britain's history began.

Portchester Castle, near Portsmouth, is a Saxon Shore Fort, where 16 of the 20 Roman towers are still standing.

Timeline

55 BC	Roman general Julius Caesar sends an expedition to Britain.
54 BC	Julius Caesar sends a second expedition to Britain.

AD 43	Romans invade Britain under Emperor Claudius; Londinium (London) begins as a Roman settlement and eventually becomes the capital of Roman Britain.
AD 45	Work on the first major Roman road in Britain begins. It is known today as Watling Street.
AD 47	Romans control most of southern and central Britain.
AD 60	Romans capture the island of Anglesey, in north-west Wales.
AD 60–61	British Queen Boudicca leads a rebellion of British tribes; the Romans defeat her in battle.
AD 70	A temple and baths are built at Aquae Sulis (Bath).
AD 70s	The Romans build an amphitheatre at Deva (Chester).
AD 74	Work begins on Caerleon, a Roman fortress in southern Wales.
AD 90	The Roman city of Viroconium (Wroxeter) is founded.
AD 118	Tribes in northern Britain rebel and are defeated by the Romans.
AD 122	Construction begins on Hadrian's Wall.
AD 142	Work on the Antonine Wall begins.
AD 155	A theatre is built at Verulamium (St Albans).
AD 200	A grand villa is built at Bignor, West Sussex.
AD 250s	Roman soldiers begin to leave Britain; Saxon raiders start to arrive.
AD 270	A fort is built at Portchester to defend Britain from Saxon invaders; it is one of 11 Saxon Shore Forts.
AD 410	The last group of Roman soldiers leaves; Britain's Roman period ends.

The remains of a Roman temple at Lydney, Gloucestershire.

Glossary

amphitheatre open-air building for shows, such as gladiator contests

archaeologist person who learns about the past by digging up old buildings or objects and studying them

conquer defeat and take control of an enemy

emperor male ruler of a country or group of countries

expedition journey made for a particular reason

fortress large fort or castle that is protected against attack

forum marketplace or public meeting area in a town

frontier far edge of a settled area, where few people live

gladiator man in ancient Rome who fought other men or wild animals, often to the death, in order to provide entertainment

legion main unit of the Roman army with about 5,000 soldiers

legionary soldier belonging to a Roman legion

merchant someone who buys and sells goods for profit

mosaic picture made of tiny pieces of stone, glass or tile

orchestra performance area at a theatre

rebellion fight against the people in charge

Roman Empire lands across Europe, North Africa and the Middle East that were under Roman control

Saxon member of a group of people from northern Europe

spring water that rises to the surface from an underground source

tribute money paid by one government to another for protection or other reasons

villa large, fancy house, especially one in the country

watchtower tower for a lookout

writing tablet thin piece of wood that the Romans used for sending written messages and letters

Find out more

BOOKS

Boudica and the Celts (History Starting Points), David Gill (Franklin Watts, 2016)

Life in Roman Britain (A Child's History of Britain), Anita Ganeri (Raintree, 2014)

Roman Britain (History of Britain), Ruth Brocklehurst and Abigail Wheatley (Usborne Publishing, 2015)

The Romans (Britain in the Past), Moira Butterfield (Franklin Watts, 2015)

WEBSITES

www.antoninewall.org/about-the-wall/the-romans-in-scotland
Find out all about the Romans in Scotland and the Antonine Wall.

www.bbc.co.uk/education/clips/zdgrkqt
Learn about Roman roads in Britain with this BBC video.

www.bbc.co.uk/education/clips/zk7xyrd
Find out what it was like for childrn children growing up in Roman Britain.

www.bbc.co.uk/education/topics/zwmpfg8
Go back in time and find out what Britain was like when the Romans were here.

www.dkfindout.com/uk/history/ancient-rome/hadrian/
This site tells all about Hadrian and his wall.

http://kids.britannica.com/kids/article/Boudicca/442493
Discover facts about Boudicca, the female warrior who tried to defeat the Romans.

PLACES TO VISIT

Antonine Wall and Rough Castle Roman Fort
near Tamfourhill, Falkirk, Scotland, FK1 4RS

Bath Roman Baths
Stall Street, Bath, BA1 1LZ

Bignor Roman Villa
Bignor, Pulborough, West Sussex, RH20 1PH

Caerleon Roman Fortress
High Street, Newport, Wales, NP18 1AE

Chester Roman Amphitheatre
Chester, CH1 2BN

Hadrian's Wall and Housesteads Roman Fort
Near Bardon Mill, Hexham, Northumberland, NE47 6NW

Portchester Castle / Saxon Shore Fort
Church Road, Portchester, Hampshire, PO16 9QW

Richborough Roman Fort
Richborough Road, Sandwich, Kent, CT13 9JW

St Albans Roman Theatre
Bluehouse Hill, St Albans, Hertfordshire, AL3 6AE

Vindolanda Roman Fort
Bardon Mill, Hexham, Northumberland, NE47 7JN

Wroxeter Roman City
Wroxeter, near Shrewsbury, Shropshire, SY5 6PH

Index